The
Golden
Hour

The
Golden
Hour

Sue Ellen
Thompson

Autumn House
Press

PITTSBURGH

Autumn House Press Staff
Executive Director: Michael Simms
Community Outreach Director: Michael Wurster
Co-Director: Eva Simms
Technology Consultant: Matthew Hamman
Editorial Consultant: Ziggy Edwards
Media Consultant: Jan Beatty
Tech Crew Chief: Mike Milberger

Jack Wolford (1945-2005)

ISBN: 1932870105
Library of Congress Control Number: 2006922104

*...for minutes at a time he shines
before he dies.*

—Sharon Olds, "The Lumens"

for my mother,
Eleanor Bromley Thompson
(1923-2002)

Table of Contents

III

Acknowledgments

Bellevue Literary Review: "The Golden Hour"

Caduceus: "Surgery in Winter"

Comstock Review: "Orthodontist Days"

Connecticut Review: "A Second Opinion," "The Visiting Nurse," "Body English"

Inkwell: "Fast Food"

Kalliope: "Helping My Daughter Move into Her First Apartment"

Missouri Review: "Happiness," "Only Child," "My Parents' Sex Life," "What She Wanted," "Babies," "Hospital Days"

Nimrod: "April 1943," "April 1993," "Leaving the Oncology Clinic with My Mother," "The Blue Blanket," "Letting Go," "In Praise of Cancer," "Terminal Math," "Closing Up the Cottage," "No Children, No Pets"

"The Blue Blanket," "The Golden Hour," "Leaving the Oncology Clinic with My Mother," "Letting Go," "In Praise of Cancer," "My Parents' Sex Life," and "A Second Opinion" won the 2003 Nimrod/ Hardman Awards/Pablo Neruda Prize in Poetry. "The Blue Blanket" was read by Garrison Keillor on "The Writer's Almanac," produced by Minnesota Public Radio and broadcast nationally March 23, 2005. "Body English" appeared in *Best American Poetry 2006*, edited by Billy Collins (Scribner, 2006).

I

In Praise of Cancer

For giving her those first six weeks
of summer, doing crosswords on the porch
in a kimono worn so thin the morning light

and birdsong could move through it. For drowsy
afternoons in chemo, reading magazines,
and for the nurses who could slip a needle

underneath the paper of her skin as easily
as a lover's name into a conversation.
For allowing us to see her as a girl again,

a stringbean, then a downy-headed infant,
curling in upon herself for sleep, and finally
as something luminous, desiring. For sending us

the unseasonable snow that dawdled
in the autumn foliage the day we drove
through the White Mountains past

Robert Frost's house, pausing long enough
for her to say, *And that has made all
the difference*. For the afternoon I brought her

home, exhausted, from the hospital and laid
her down to nap on that same porch—
the screens dissolving now in late

October's radiance—and for the sleep
she sank into so gratefully a smile
shone like water on her thin, dry lips.

For taking what it had to take so casually
at first—an appetite for olives, windfall
hair. For being quick and greedy at the end.

April 1943

Why did they marry? We had heard
the story a hundred times: She was on spring
break; he was stationed in Texas, learning
how to fly a B-24. But things

got a little murky after that.
He met her at the train, having thought
of everything— a motel room, a ring—but in what
order? Indignation. A little sweet-talk.

The rector of St. Paul's-on-the-Plains made
an exception to his rule about marrying young
military couples. He liked the way
my father's hand on her neck kept the sun

off. Why did they marry? For love, of course.
Although back then they called it "the War."

Happiness

When we were young, it came to us
unbidden, slipping its weightless arm
around our shoulders, urging us toward
the light that shimmered all around. Remember
the paneled bedroom of our first
apartment? We'd just come from
the beach, my day-glo orange bikini
radiating, still, a kind of heat.
You spread me on a mattress
thinly buttered by a sheet, and when I rose
again, it wasn't with the weight of flesh
but like the gauzy curtain, billowed
by the wind, through which we glimpsed
the mower's progress through the tresses
of the next-door-neighbor's lawn.

In middle age, it has a heft to it
and something chilly at the margins,
like a good fur coat whose satin lining
shoots a warning down the sleeve. Each time
I feel its husk begin to stir in me,
I think of how the sun, in just a few years,
turned that flimsy drape to dust. That's
why people cry at weddings, isn't it? Because
the happy couple's happiness is something
we have all been lofted by, just as we've seen
the mower, intent upon his work.

Dr. Colin Simms

We were living in England, where for fourteen
weeks I didn't know I was pregnant. Then
I rolled over in bed one morning
and felt a fist beneath me. My boyfriend

was in the upstairs bathroom, taking a shower.
An American acquaintance persuaded her doctor to meet
with us the next day. We took the Underground,
thrilled and silenced by the possibility.

There was an open fire at one end of the room,
a Persian rug and, behind his desk, a bay
window overlooking Harley Street. Afternoon
tea was served, and he called us by my maiden name.

Slipping behind a lacquered screen, I undressed.
Then he examined me: *Oh my yes.*

Happiness

Three of us, our bodies like plums, jostled
by childbirth, our infant daughters
afloat on rafts of flannel in the grass.
Spring sun warmed the garden slates,
the wooden bench on which we sat,
while down the street a mower thrummed
but came no closer. Our lives were tethered
to a sodden diaper in a pastel sleeper,
the work we'd left unfinished languished
just beyond our seeing. One
of us would hear her baby cry and peel
a triangle of blouse back, while the other two
would sit there sipping iced tea, nipples burning.

Someone should have stopped his car
and rolled his window down,
he should have shouted at us, *This
is happiness!* Someone should have held
us there until the mower's purr, the sun-
warmed wood, the fine gold infant-hair the breeze
made lift and fall like insect wings
had entered into us and formed
a kind of knowledge we could store
against such days as we have now.

Mary Lou divorced and moved away,
while Kate's breast felt the tug of cancer,
followed by her sternum, spine, and hips.
I had a camera in my purse that day,
I should have made them smile into the sun's
fierce radiance until the tears tattooed their cheeks.
Then we would have it framed in silver, here
among the hushed and polished vacancies
of our heated, well-lit houses.

Ghost Telegram

There were three telegrams, but only two
were real. My mother thought she saw
the first one waiting on the front stoop
when she came home from the movies in 1944.

The next morning, there was a real one:
THE SECRETARY OF WAR DESIRES ME TO EXPRESS
HIS DEEP REGRET...MISSING IN ACTION
OVER ITALY. Seven weeks crept

by. Then someone intercepted an unofficial
short wave radio broadcast that referred
to 2nd Lt. Elliott Thompson as a prisoner
of war in Germany. That was the third.

She still had a husband, it seemed:
Imagine not knowing for seven weeks.

My Father Gets His Wish

1 For years my father had longed to be
2 like the men he'd seen in the ads on t.v.,
3 recumbent in their La-Z-Boy recliners.
4 He'd tell my mother in all honesty

5 there were few things that could make
6 an old man happy. With that, he'd slink
7 off to the living room, which was arranged
8 exactly like the one she'd seen

9 in *Country Living,* with wing chairs anchoring
10 a reproduction oriental and a Queen
11 Anne coffee table tiled with magazines.
12 After our first visit from Hospice,

13 when my mother found out she'd have to rearrange
14 her bedroom's furniture to accommodate
15 the hospital bed she'd sworn would never take
16 the place of her canopied, pencil-post antique,

17 she said that when his birthday came,
18 I should buy my father a recliner. She
19 had begun to see our lives continuing
20 without her, and she wanted them to be

21 just like the old lives, but blessed by everything
22 to which she'd been an obstacle. As she signed
23 the check, I watched the horses from the neighboring
24 farm raise their fluent heads as one

25 and, summoned by the invisible, move in unison
26 towards an opening in the pasture fence,
27 while a brisk wind closed the gate behind them.

Prisoner of War

He pried loose boards from the walls and floor
to burn in the barracks stove when the chips of coal
ran out. His only clothing was the uniform
he was shot down in, and the Baltic cold

was unrelenting. They killed his bombardier
when, without thinking, he ran out
to catch a fly ball and hit the wire.
The day they expanded the prison compound

to make room for newcomers, my father saw
several yards of untrampled earth to the south.
He tore out handfuls of fresh, raw
onion grass and stuffed it in his mouth.

Doing swell, his letters to my mother said.
Don't worry your pretty little head.

The Man Show

My husband cooks my dinner,
irons his own shirts, and on the first night
home in bed after a week of traveling
wants only to fold himself around me
like an envelope. So when
"The Man Show" ad appears
in our local paper—an arena-sized display
of trucks with elevated frames
and bloated tires, motorcycles polished
to a family silver gleam,
and guest appearances by Miss
Connecticut, Miss March,
Miss Played-a-Small-Supporting-Role-in-*Baywatch*-Once—
I know that he would rather pop
a bottle of Italian red, open
his Tuscan cookbook and,
while sage's silver drifts
among the cannellini beans, sit
intricately twined with me watching
Out of Africa again—that scene
where Robert Redford cooks a meal
for Meryl Streep out on the moonlit savannah.

My favorite scene comes at the end
of my mother's illness: She is bald
and sparrow-thin, pinned
to the bed by one sharp hip,
head bent to the work of dying.
Outside, an unseasonable snow
moves quietly among the burning maples.
Mom, look, I say, but she cannot raise
her hatchling's gaze to the level
of the window. Then my father
scurries in, carrying golden broth
of sun and snowflakes on a cracker.

The American Hotel

We caught a bargain flight to Amsterdam
from our chilly flat in London for a honeymoon.
The hotel clerk didn't understand
English, and we found ourselves in a room

with twin beds. Should we complain?
I had a fever and a sore throat,
and we'd been living together for seven
years. Then I remembered my mother's boast

that she and my father had never spent a night
apart. As she dozed off during those final days
of her illness, my father would be curled beside
her, sunlight setting the bed ablaze.

Never sleep apart if you have a choice:
My mother's words, in my mother's voice.

1

Blue

My husband gave me paperweights
as gifts when we were young: glass heart,
a globe across whose surface lakes
and rivers swirled darkly, and a triangular

one where three strands tangled in a burst
of color at the top. Each tried to say
something he couldn't—*Don't hurt
me. Come with me. We should have a baby.*

Then I was lost to him for a while,
and rather than making me feel like a criminal,
he let me drift back on my own and find
it on my desk: a pyramid of cobalt

through which light passed and was eloquent.
So this was what "blue" really meant.

Stillbirth

A miracle, but one too commonplace
to mention. My mother would go
up to the cedar room in the attic one day
and bring down her maternity clothes.

Then she would stop eating, and start up
again, and it didn't matter whether she ate
or not, because soon she would have a stomach
on which she could rest her dinner plate.

After her fourth, a strange thing happened:
She and my father disappeared
in the middle of the night. She came home thin
and followed the bassinet back upstairs

to the attic. The shapeless dresses were put away,
and no one had anything more to say.

11 Park Vista

We rented a room from an English violinist
and shared the kitchen that filled the second floor.
We had until the lessons downstairs were finished
to cook and eat our dinner before

he started his. Married now
and beginning to show, I took the train
to London every day and joined the crowd
perched on folding camp-stools at the Tate.

Returning one evening, I saw my husband
wreathed in steam above the kitchen stove
while a young girl raised her violin
and released a flock of sparrows in the parlor below.

I paused on the front walk, breathless with greed.
Food, music, children—all within reach.

Fast Food

When the doctor prescribed a liquid called Megace,
designed to elicit an appetite where hers
had waned to a crescent, it made my mother crave
the foods she'd spent a lifetime avoiding.
She'd lift the lid and start licking her fingers
before we had cleared the parking lot
at Kentucky Fried Chicken, and once
she made me drive straight from her CAT-scan
to Burger King, where she downed a Whopper
with extra cheese and more delight
than she'd ever displayed at Thanksgiving.
After raising a shake made with real
ice cream to her face, she closed
her eyes reverently and shaved her moustache
with a finger. On our way home from chemotherapy,

she made me stop at McDonald's for lunch,
and with the same bliss-driven spiritedness
said she wanted a picnic. The sky had been lowering
its hopes all day, but we found a grassy place
on the banks of the Merrimack. Propped
by a damp stone, lichen-stained, she devoured
her paper-wrapped feast. Her hair—
which would fall like the leaves of the willow
behind her in just one week—caught the mist
that rose like a thought of rain in the mind of the heavens.
It formed a loose cloud around her face,
bathed in silvery pleasure. She held
a crisp sickle of fry aloft and gazed
at its tip, dripping in rich red ketchup.
What could be better than this? she asked,
and indeed, I could think of nothing.

Sewing

The night before my older sister's wedding,
my mother and I sat up late
hand-stitching a little cloud of netting
to the brim of each bridesmaid's hat.

To be alone with her was so rare
I couldn't think of what I had to say.
We worked in silence beneath the chandelier
until it was almost daybreak.

Soon I'd have a room of my own
and she would only be cooking for six.
We drifted among the wreaths we had sewn,
nursing quietly on our fingertips.

That she still had me was a comfort,
I think. And I still had her.

Happiness

My daughter and I spent a morning painting
portraits of Albert, her teddy bear,
who posed on the bed for hours without complaining,
meeting our efforts with his indifferent stare.

As an artist, I hadn't progressed
since grade school, but she was only four
and marveled at the confidence with which I sketched
his shapeless limbs. What could be more

thrilling than to possess a genius in her eyes
for something at which I was clearly mediocre?
In fifteen years I'd realize
that her talent was vast, mine local.

But "happiness" is what I still define
as those days when all the gifts were mine.

The Golden Hour

Those final weeks, there was an hour
each afternoon when stillness would conspire
with the autumn light. They would embrace

my mother in her sickbed
and my father with his book spread-eagled
on his chest beside her, dozing.

I'd stand outside their bedroom door
and know that nothing bad would happen for an hour—
that I could leave the house, return to find

the cat still curled between the shapes
that were my parents and the same
staccato puffs of air escaping from my mother's

lips. I'd walk the fields behind
their house, the endless avenues of dry
golden cornstalks leading nowhere and away,

and think of those first few weeks at home
with my infant daughter, how the world I'd known
before, the world of books and men and dinner

parties, had abandoned me. The phone calls
from my friends at work dropped off
and what remained of my life gazed at me with slate

blue eyes. Once, after nursing, she fell
into a sleep so bottomless the cell
door opened briefly and I thought

of slipping out, but her hold on me was already
too fierce. Pausing mid-field, I'd turn instinctively
back toward that slowly stirring maelstrom

of grief. My mother would awaken to the sound
of a November wind quickening around
the corners of the house and the sun dropping into

its coinbox. Sometimes her eyes
would flutter briefly, and I'd remember why
I kept that child so close to me for years

and how relinquishing her came hard.
The hour would end. I'd put my mother's arms
around my neck and lift her to the commode.

I'd rent a Katharine Hepburn video
and re-heat leftovers. If it was cold,
I'd swaddle her in afghans on the sofa.

My Parents' Sex Life

I never asked my mother when
her periods stopped, or if she'd ever been
unfaithful, or what exactly happened
to the baby she'd been taken to the hospital
to have in 1955. She came home
thin again, the house fell silent, and the urge
to know more passed. Nor did I ask

what happens to sex after fifty years.
Straightening their bed one day,
I found the cat-shaped cushion
my father kept between his knees while sleeping
to prevent one leg from cutting circulation
in the other. My mother blushed and said,
Your father's pussy pillow. I shied away

from their private joke. The week before
my mother started chemotherapy,
a nurse in her late thirties sat us down
to review the ground rules: No more wine
with dinner, flush the toilet twice each time
you pee, and make sure you use condoms—
at which my mother smiled beatifically

and said, *We've taken care of that.*
It was then the stand of evergreens
that had marked the boundary between
her life and mine turned dry as tinder
and began their vanishing. Death, which until now
had been remote and slumbering, gathered
its belongings up and started moving toward me.

II

First Trimester

I did everything you're not supposed to:
Waiting to meet my husband after work,
I drank at the pub every afternoon—
pint after pint of foamy lager.

Then I got shingles—a cummerbund
of angry blisters caused by inflamed
nerve endings—and followed the advice of someone
who suggested marijuana for the pain.

So when the baby was born, I checked first
for toes and fingers, and thought we were out of the woods
when the doctor pronounced her "perfect."
Throughout her golden childhood

I thought of her as strong-willed, spirited.
The woods lay dark and deep ahead.

Orthodontist Days

What I remember is the silence, which would fall
somewhere between the airlock of the outer doors

and our emergence from the elevator, as if an old
tarpaulin, lashed by winter storms, had settled

over us, Dr. Kozlowski's waiting room aswim
in mildew-colored light. My daughter

wouldn't speak to me or read a magazine,
she'd sit there with her baseball cap pulled low

over her forehead and a fist jammed tight
in either armpit, feigning sleep, although one sneaker

never ceased its restless motion. It was here
I felt our distance at its most acute, an empty chair

between us where she'd fling her jacket down
when Dr. K. appeared and held the door ajar

so she could pass between my suffering
and her own. Those Thursdays were the tail end

of a bleak affair, when words lose all
but their capacity to wound. So I let

that silence bear us onward: Better
to be in its thrall than cast out on my own.

Five Kids

My mother claimed she could tell us apart
by the sound of our peeing. Lying in bed, she knew
my older sister's bossy gush, the spurts
of impatience from my younger sister, the altitude-

induced tonal differences of the two boys.
She said my pee was tentative
and ladylike, something I enjoyed
hearing because I was neither. If I was sick

in the middle of the night and cried out "Mom!"
at the crescendo of my retching—something I still do,
in my head—she'd be at my side already, with her "I'm
here, honey" and the right toothbrush.

As for my only child, my daughter?
I think I don't know half as much about her.

Guns

None of the mothers I knew would let
their children play with toy guns.
But my father, blind to parental etiquette
and longing for a grandson, carved my daughter one

out of wood. It might have been in deference
to her grandfather's handmade gift
or in the belief that she was incapable of violence
that I allowed her to carry it

in the waistband of her shorts. I had yet
to glimpse the defiant nature that would begin
to manifest itself in a few years, or to suspect
that the woman she would become—vegan,

anti-consumer, politically active—required
a weapon, or that I would be caught in the crossfire.

Surgery in Winter

After I know it's not cancer, after
I start believing the scar will recede
to a flat white seam, my husband
makes me French toast with sourdough bread
soaked in egg, cooked in butter, set
in a sweet amber moat and I feel
our old life seeping up like spring rain
from the roots of the grasses to make
something green at the tip. He holds

me up at the waist as I stand in the shower,
then unfolds my towel, pressing its thirst
to my hollows and runnels and slopes.
I sit on the bed as he aims the blow-dryer's
hot blast straight downward, bowing my head
as he lifts the limp strands to the heat.

Later, he pushes my heels into hiking boots,
tightening the laces and tying the bow
in a bow. Then he teaches me how
to move forward, guiding me through
the rough chop of floorboards and doorsills,
into a world whose dangers
he's quelled and battened with snow.

A Second Opinion

Because none of them had touched her yet—
aside from the random palm laid flat
upon her tumored abdomen—
when Doctor Meadows made a D-ring
with his hand around my mother's wrist
she fell for him, no matter that her first
impression had been of someone slightly
vain, his crossed leg in its dress sock
descending to a graceful arch,
his narrow foot like mangrove rising
from the marsh of an Italian loafer.
He reached across the corner of his desk,
and with one finger on the porcelain knob
of her wristbone, rubbed his thumb
against the current of her racing pulse.

You realize, Mrs. Thompson, this disease
will take your life, he said, to which
my mother murmured *Yes*
in the rapt and breathless way
that women have when men who are beyond
their wildest dreams decide to pay
them some attention. Observing this,
I understood what *bedside manner* means,
and for the first time thought of it
as having to do not so much with kindness
as with a willingness to be
here at this place of immense and frightening delicacy.

Wallpapering

My parents argued over wallpaper. Would stripes
make the room look larger? He
would measure, cut, and paste; she'd swipe
the flaws out with her brush. Once it was properly

hung, doubt would set in. Would the floral
have been a better choice? Then it would grow
until she was certain: it had to go. Divorce
terrified me as a child. I didn't know

what led to it, but I had my suspicions.
The stripes came down. Up went
the flowers. Eventually it became my definition
of marriage: bad choices, arguments

whose victors time refused to tell,
but everything done together and done well.

Hospital Days

The tests, the bloodwork—they
were good days, with magazines
to absorb the time spent waiting.
The nurses' banter spread a sheen
of normalcy over everything,
and the doctors left a little space
in their advice where spirit
might lodge. The three of us
went everywhere together, and at last
I knew the pleasure that the only child
takes in the company of her makers.

Then the doctor came to us one day
and said the chemo hadn't made
the kind of progress he was looking for,
that we could take my mother home
and stay. We sat there, stunned by what
our weeks of rushing to appointments
had not left us time to contemplate,
then drove home without speaking. This day,
unlike the others, would not end
with smiles and good-byes, my father's
and my arms tucked beneath my mother's
and hope's modest, steady flame
still unextinguished in us at the thought
of eating supper at the kitchen table
before we called the cats in from the dark.

Frieda and Jules

They drove their caravan from the Netherlands
to the maritime museum conference every year:
Mijnheer and Mevrouw Jules von Beylen
with their blue smocks and milk-white hair.

They cooked their meals on a camp stove
and ate on folding chairs beside a succession
of European harbors. They took turns dozing
on each other's shoulders during lectures.

The last time we saw them was in Sweden
after a rough crossing during which we were comforted
by the immensely calm, beatific Frieda,
Jules curled in her lap like a fiddlehead.

That night, I awoke with a raging thirst,
wondering which one of us would die first.

April 1993

My parents were getting ready to celebrate
their fiftieth anniversary. "A family cruise,"
my brother suggested. "A compound at the lake"—
this from my sister. It was all a ruse,

the whole point being to invite us
on a free vacation. They let us talk.
Then my mother, her voice stripped by laryngitis
to its truest, most essential notes, locked

eyes with my father as she said, "It's all decided."
They booked the honeymoon suite on the *Delta Queen*
and watched, from their stateroom window, starboard side,
the West unfurl. I don't believe

they thought of us once, but only of the vast
country around them, in which they were alone at last.

Letting Go

Throughout my mother's illness, friends
kept telling me that when her time came,
she would need permission from me to depart
for the vast white snows of death.

So I drove north frantically that final night,
great gulps of highway disappearing
down the station wagon's open throat,
arriving not to uniforms and flashing lights

but to a house so nearly dark I thought
she might have tired of waiting. A single
small lamp struggled in the furthest corner
of the room, its gaunt light faltering

just inches from the thick, cut-paper
shade. I climbed in bed with her and listened
as my own quick breathing calmed,
then hers did, just before it tapered

to a halt. Years ago I'd gone home, spurned
by a lover she never knew I'd had. She fed me,
washed my clothes, while I drew closer to my own
despair. She didn't have to say a word.

Depressive

He was "moody." We were young and, I thought,
happy, but something dark would reach
up and pull him under, even as I fought
to save him. I would plead

for an explanation. He had none.
So I moved into the spare room one day
while he was installing an exhibit on celestial navigation
at the museum. We continued this way

for a week. Then one evening I walked
into the apartment to find the doors to my bastion
and all the rooms, except our bedroom, blocked
by velvet ropes between brass stanchions.

I measured my love's arc and elevation
and moved back in without explaining.

Sorry Hour

He mixes his manhattan with a chopstick, switches
on the evening news: Soldiers bidding
farewell to their families, a sadness he has known.
He shared this hour with his wife
for 60 years: They squandered it at will,
sifting through the day's accomplishments
as the sun eased comfortably behind the hill.

The Beltway Sniper's at it again. Consumed
as if by fire, those decades vanish. The room
remains, this hour's habit, the table
and her empty chair. There's been
an accident—a local family has lost both sons.
He wishes he could weep for them,
and is ashamed when his loss becomes

briefly bearable. He checks his watch,
refills his glass. He was a prisoner of war
their first two years of marriage. Why shouldn't
someone else's tragedy outshine his own?
He strains the liquor carefully between
the chilled glass and his bridgework,
drawing solace through another's grief.

Depressive

I made excuses for his being
the way he was. I'd tell our daughter,
"Dad's under a lot of pressure at the museum,"
or, "He didn't mean it; you ought to

be more forgiving." But when he slipped
beyond our reach, I'd abandon
him to his own darkness and take ownership
of the house. I'd be cheerful, accommodating, a paragon

of the virtues he lacked. I'd vacuum,
scrub, and polish as if he weren't there
in our midst, spreading his bleak perfume.
Then, when I could no longer bear

it, I'd take to my bed and weep.
He'd be downstairs, watching TV.

The Visiting Nurse

A lacrosse coach's face and a ponytail
thick as my forearm, laced with blond. She said
she'd earned her nursing degree at Yale,
just an hour west of the life I'd led.
She married a doctor and moved up North
so he could establish a hometown practice.
With girlish loops she filled out her forms,
then proffered the dreaded word: *hospice.*

She knew her way out. But before she left,
she turned and embraced me in a crush
of Gore-Tex. I gave myself to her and wept.
I had endured every courtesy up
to this point in my mother's illness,
but I could not bear her prodigal kindness.

Average

My father rated everything on a scale
of 1 to 10. At a restaurant, when the waitress
wanted to know if he'd enjoyed his meal,
he'd say, "I'd give it a 6"—

which meant, "Better than average, but there
are lots of restaurants, and who's to say
that I won't find one where
they have an even better strawberry shortcake?"

Three years after my mother died,
he asked me how I'd rate my marriage.
Things were good. I gave it a 9.
He looked at me as if I'd called it "average."

"I'm sorry for you," he said, as tears swelled
in his eyes. "I would have given mine a 12."

Leaning In

Sometimes, in the middle of a crowded store on a Saturday
afternoon, my husband will rest his hand
on my neck, or on the soft flesh belted at my waist,
and pull me to him. I understand

his question: Why are we so fortunate
when all around us, friends are falling prey
to divorce and illness? It seems intemperate
to celebrate in a more conspicuous way

so we just stand there, leaning in
to one another, until that moment
of sheer blessedness dissolves and our skin,
which has been touching, cools and relents,

settling back into our separate skeletons
as we head toward Housewares to resume our errands.

Body English

I'd seen a golfer's body curve
into a deep parenthesis as the ball
inched toward the cup, and I knew
how mothers in the bleachers leaned
and flapped their useless wings
when their child's kick arced perfectly
before descending shy of the goal.
As the two men from the funeral home
maneuvered my mother's body
through the narrow, sloping hallways
of her eighteenth century cape
to where the black van had reversed its way
up the steep slope to the porch,
I cowered with my father and my sister
in a distant bedroom, waiting
for their footsteps and the thumps
against the woodwork to abate.
Through a narrow opening in the door
that centuries of weather had warped
so that the latch no longer fit
we glimpsed the stretcher as they carried it
across the porch. *Alley-oop!* one said
as the other raised my mother's bare feet
high, letting her head, so newly sprouted
with winter wheat, tilt dangerously
downward. Suddenly the three of us
were on our feet—bodies craned,
chins lifted skyward—as if by pitching
all our weight we could prevent
the next bad thing from happening.

Tree

Snapped off mid-trunk, too far
from the ground to free
and haul away, it lay
in a collapse of limbs.
Circling it uneasily—
if weather could fell
a tree this strong, then who
among us was safe?—I noticed
the breath that seemed
still to be moving through it.

A breeze came along and lifted
its leaves like ears
to a conversation. It appeared—
was this possible?—eager
to speak: heaved up and leaning
toward me. Then it simply
lay back on its bed of lawn,
its green gone ashen and mortal.
It had exalted itself one final time:
So it was with my mother.

Leaving the Oncology Clinic with My Mother

We stop at a department store, lured
reflexively by signs proclaiming *End*

of Summer Sale on Now! The air
inside is cool and motionless, she spots a pair

of slim black loafers. Yes,
they're perfect, we agree: a dozen ounces

of the softest leather, soles so thin
that through them she'll read everything

the earth has written. We pay the clerk
and, for several minutes afterward,

she's light again and free to roam, equipped
with all she needs to make this final trip.

Dr. Crow

We'd hoped that the oncologist would be
an older man, someone who awoke
this morning with a twinge beneath
the cushion of his hip and thought

it might be kidney—someone who had seen
the worst so often he would be imbued
with it and radiate the feeling that it's normal
to be dying, that like the coach whose job it is

to train with you the first few miles,
dropping back while you complete the final
laps, he's just a step behind you. But Dr. Crow
is young, with dark hair laid like feathers,

shining and impervious, a crisp
white shirt and lipstick-colored tie.
My mother lies on the examining table
while he presses one hand lightly down

upon the other, roaming casually
among the foothills of her liver before telling us
he's seen the radiology and doesn't think
there's much that he can do. My parents nod,

I nod, all the while noticing his khakis,
how the heavy cotton hangs from his slim waist
and narrow woven belt, their creases breaking
slightly at his kneecaps before falling

to his bare, tanned, sandaled feet.
My parents rise and thank him for his honesty.
I thank him, too—not knowing why until,
cradling my mother's elbow like a teacup

in my palm, I cross the scalding asphalt
and feel heat burst suddenly from the sealed,
parked car. And then it comes to me:
I'm not the one who's dying.

III

What She Wanted

When my mother realized there were things
she'd never do again—things she loved,
like grocery shopping, making beds,
and going to the mall each winter morning
to walk a few brisk indoor miles with her friends—
she took it in without acknowledging
her loss, or giving any outward sign
that these were privileges for which
she'd gladly bargain. Each day became
its own farewell, as one by one
her gifts were taken from her—hair,
the strength to walk unaided,
then one day she sat before her open
checkbook, utterly unable to complete
the small, deft moves required
to pay the cleaning lady. That night,

I listened as she struggled to the bathroom
with her walker, its syncopated thumps
as reassuring now as footsteps.
When she fell, I found her folded
in the space between the toilet's vast
white porcelain machinery and the sink's
chilled pedestal. Her head was bald,
her nightgown thin, it seemed
there was so little left that could be taken
from her. At breakfast the next morning
she made figure eights in oatmeal.
Mom, what would you like to do today?
I asked, desperate to erase the long
night's losses. Her lashless eyes were dull
with longing as she said, *I want to run a race.*

Babies

Once I had my own, I found
other people's only mildly interesting
in comparison. Why were they so proud
of their run-of-the-mill offspring?

Then mine left the house sweet
one day and returned a simmering adolescent.
In the years that followed, I'd meet
a mother with a stroller wearing that expression

that combines being hopelessly in love with being
desperately needed and avert my gaze,
knowing what lay ahead. Cleaning
my daughter's vacant room today,

I wondered if mothering had ever been my style.
Then, just as suddenly, I wanted a grandchild.

Terminal Math

At the end of a lifetime
in which she'd done
nothing more to augment her looks
than pat down her face
with some powder,
my mother asked me if I
would tweeze her eyebrows.
Two months of chemo
had already claimed
her gray-blond frizz
and her lashes were gone
in what seemed like
a blink. What percentage lay
in deducting these last
few hairs from a body
already canceling itself?
She must have believed
that in ministering to what
remained, she could balance
the equation.

So I counted
the fine brown hairs
that traced her brow
and thought about what
I could do to improve
their distribution.
With her head in my lap
on the sunlit porch
and her gaze diluted
in blissful trust,
I braced my hand
against her skull
and started subtracting.

Magnolia

A lush magnolia—whose pink blooms,
when they fell, were slick as banana peels—
would break into flower outside my daughter's room
on her April birthday every year.

It marked the beginning of something when she was young:
We'd lie on her bed that first spring night
and leave the window open to the hands that flung
palmfuls of pinkness down in the moonlight.

When she was seventeen, riddled with anger
and eager to be done with me, the tree began
to fail. Planted in a corner, its roots tangled
in upon themselves in a way that seemed human.

By the time she left home, it was dead.
It didn't die. It was strangled, she said.

Closing Up the Cottage

Brightening at the prospect of an outing,
my mother let us gather her from where
she had been scattered by her illness.
Inch by inch she picked her way
across the lawn to where the car sat,
idling. My husband drove
while I stared hard at the undressed
landscape and my father made
the whooshing sound with which he'd filled
the rifts in conversation since
he gave up cigarettes. Once there,
we propped and cushioned her
in a wicker armchair, where she sat enthroned
like a child-queen, thin legs dangling
just above the floorboards.

As we went about the task of shutting out
a season we'd already brought indoors,
she seemed uncommonly alert
to her surroundings, as if she knew
this was the last she'd see of the world
beyond the room of her disease.
She took it all in—every molecule of light
that tumbled free when screens were lifted
from their hinges, every leaf that danced
in the heaped-up corners of the yard,
the gulping sound that water in the pipes made
on its final journey to the hard clay underground.
I like it here was all she said
that I remember—that, and how,
when we brought her home, we carried her
in a sedan-chair made of arms and elbows,
my father scurrying behind us
with his sweeping sound, closing
and then locking every door.

Helping My Daughter Move into Her First Apartment

This is all I am to her now:
a pair of legs in running shoes,

two arms strung with braided wire.
She heaves a carton sagging with CDs

at me and I accept it gladly, lifting
with my legs, not bending over,

raising each foot high enough
to clear the step. Fortunate to be

of any use to her at all,
I wrestle, stooped and single-handed,

with her mattress in the stairwell,
saying nothing as it pins me,

sweating, to the wall. Vacuum cleaner,
spiny cactus, five-pound sacks

of rice and lentils slumped
against my heart: up one flight

of stairs and then another,
down again with nothing in my arms.

Reading My Mother's Journals

She kept track of birthdays for decades
after their rightful owners had died.
"My mother would have been 105
today," her entry for March 10th reads,

although she lost her mother when she was 12,
in 1935. "Ginna and Charlie's 64th
anniversary," she writes of an aunt who divorced
when I was a teenager. I've found myself

doing the same thing since the night
of her death. Today, for instance, marks
61 years since she departed
by train for Texas, where my father was in flight

school during the war. A few days
later, they were married. We live
two lives: The first in our own, original
wording, then in our children's paraphrase.

As long as I can tell it, my parents will remain
newlyweds. But now there's no one left to mourn
my grandmother, who looks forlorn
even in photographs, and whose name was Adelaide.

Questions

Did your mother love me? It seems an idle
question from an old man looking to be reassured.
After 60 years of marriage, is it possible
he's forgotten what it was to be adored?

Outright declarations of love
were never their style, although I can recall
him sneaking up behind her at the stove
and grabbing her in places that made us all

squirm with joy and embarrassment. It wasn't until
she died that doubt set in:
Did she write about him in her journals?
Did she breathe his name at the end?

There are so few fears the living can allay:
Of course she did is all I say.

Language

was our battleground, although
my mother's education had come to a halt
with marriage at 19. A typical scenario
involved a skirmish between "for-tay" and "forte"

or one-upsmanship involving "fewer"
and "less." How she loved being right,
and how I relished her discomfiture
when I was. We had our final fight

over the pronunciation of "ophthalmologist"—
she said it was "oph," not "op."
When she pulled the dictionary from its niche,
it landed like a karate chop.

She was right and so was I.
Now one of us would have to die.

Before

Off the highway in New Hampshire, air
a golden, pollen-heavy broth. Quilt
of green thrown over the mountain,
although I know of no one who is ill.

Parents waiting for me on the screened porch,
iced drinks ticking as daylight flows
from a season that feels final,
although I know of nothing ending now.

My mother winces as she rises,
pricked by her breath's insistent spear.
A quickening deep in the pit of me,
although I see no weapons anywhere.

All night the old house turns and tosses
beneath the thick black fur of summer sky.
We are not expecting anything to happen:
Why, then, the dawn's alarming eye?

No Children, No Pets

I bring the cat's body home from the vet's
in a running-shoe box held shut
with elastic bands. Then I clean
the corners where she has eaten and
slept, scrubbing the hard bits of food
from the baseboard, dumping the litter
and blasting the pan with a hose. The plastic
dishes I hide in the basement, the pee-
soaked towel I put in the trash. I put
the catnip mouse in the box and I put
the box away, too, in a deep
dirt drawer in the earth.

When the death-energy leaves me,
I go to the room where my daughter slept
in nursery school, grammar school, high school,
I lie on her milky bedspread and think
of the day I left her at college, how nothing
could keep me from gouging the melted candle-wax
out from between her floorboards,
or taking a razor blade to the decal
that said to the firemen, *Break
this window first.* I close my eyes now
and enter a place that's clearly
expecting me, swaddled in loss
and then losing that, too, as I move
from room to bone-white room
in the house of the rest of my life.

Napping

My mother, who had walked six miles,
six days a week for years, knew
that her life was ending. One day she smiled
at me and said, *I'm not in the mood*

for walking today. I think I'll take
a nap instead. She never napped
before lunch. But how else could she say
it? All morning she lay wrapped

in an afghan on the sofa, her eyes intent
upon a pattern taking shape in the air.
I cleaned her kitchen, my diligence
a substitute for grieving and a kind of prayer.

She didn't tell me not to: adrift, serene,
quietly dropping the reins of her routine.

Only Child

There were five of us, and I was number
two. My parents retired up north
to be near three and four, who were younger
and whom love drove south. Of course

there were still three of us, all
New Englanders. Then my mother got sick
and my older sister was travelling that fall
and they thought my brother's youngest might be autistic

and that left me. I never thought
I'd be steering my mother by the arm
or untangling her legs when they were crossed,
nor did I think I'd be the only guard

she'd have to slip past to die.
One child: Has it ever been otherwise?

Thanksgiving

My mother's older brothers had all died
around Thanksgiving, and perhaps because
of this, it was her favorite holiday,
a time when she could leave
her thumb-shaped signature around a pie
and think of her brother Bob,
whose favorite was mince, or sift
a little flour into the drippings and think
of her brother Paul, who always made
the gravy. The meal was a memorial
and a celebration, her own late middle age
an endless autumn. So when the doctor said

that a "modest course" of chemotherapy
might enable her to live until
Thanksgiving, there was no question
she'd go through with it. She spent
those days reclined in a vinyl-covered lounge chair
with an expression on her face of sheer,
untroubled certainty. It was clear to us
that she had set her heart on dying
in November—month when loss
seemed only natural as we gathered
in a house bereft of milk and bread and meat.

Vegan

My daughter hauls her sacks of beans
and vegetables in from the car and begins to chop.
My father, who has had enough caffeine,
makes himself a manhattan-on-the-rocks.

It's Sunday, his night for sausage and eggs,
hers for stir-fried lentils, rice, and kale.
Watching her cook eases his fatigue
and loneliness. Later, she'll trim his toenails.

He no longer has an appetite
for anything beyond this evening ritual.
But he'll fry himself an egg tonight
and eat dinner with his granddaughter. For a widower,

there is no greater comfort in the world
than his girls and his girls' girls.

The Petitioner

My mother interceded with my father
if I wanted something big—like the time
I needed his permission to squander
an entire summer's earnings on an airline

ticket to meet my boyfriend in Taipei
for R&R. *Let me talk
to him first*, she would always say.
The discussions were held behind their unlocked

door, from which she would emerge victorious.
When she died, his reputation
for authority collapsed, revealing her genius
for quietly making all the important decisions.

He wandered, stunned, through the empty house
and slept sitting up, embraced by her blouse.

Fishing on the Merrimack, My Father Sees a B-24

Dozing and drifting slowly toward Boscawen
in his battered ten-foot Alumicraft,
he hears the distant rumble of the Flying Boxcar
he and his crew named "Sack

Time Sal" for the hours of blissful rest
they coveted. They flew her over
Sicily and bombed the German base at Trieste
before bailing out 50 years ago.

Now the blunt nose and twin tail
stabilizers emerge from a low-hanging cloud,
its slow propellers pummeling the air.
Following the river from the air show south,

it labors in the shadow of the shadow cast
over my father in his frail craft.

Babies

On a plane, my mother would roam the aisles
in search of a wailing infant she could calm
by pacing up and down with him, smiling
her I'm-in-heaven smile. Or I'd come home

to find a crib set up in my room
for a neighbor's child. The top of the family pyramid
was always reserved for whoever had produced
the most recent offspring. So it was with

a sense of something not being right
that I stood up at her funeral and surveyed a sea
of aging faces in a room of unearthly quiet.
Devoted to her own and others' progeny

as she was, and as a reward for her swift dying,
couldn't there have been a baby crying?

Sixteen Months Later

Snow honeycombs and some lawn bleeds through.
A goldfinch remembers the mesh bag feeder.
March sun fills the cat's bowl,
then mine. I am unaccountably happy.

Death has lifted the heavy skirts
that have cumbered my every step forward.
I wander the yard, gathering winter debris,
for the pleasure of bending and straightening.

I thought that joy had abandoned me
for someone much younger. Now it returns
in a nest of leaves and the quick, dank breeze
that revives them. Loading the woodstove,

steeping the tea, hefting wet corduroys
from the machine to the warm embrace of the dryer.
It's all that a mother, dying or not,
could have wished for her second daughter.

Super Bowl Sunday

Why should this scene—boys
in their late teens, playing touch
football in the snow, sleeves
pushed back and forearms
strawberried with cold—
bring me to a halt, eyes
threatening to spill? The snow's
been trampled to the color of tin
on the field next to the senior citizen
housing complex, formerly
a school. Some wearing shorts
with heavy boots and one
in plaid pajama bottoms,
they hurl themselves like storms
against the January sky.
They leap, they reach, collide
and run brief distances
before they're brought to earth
and buried by their kind.
Although I cannot say
what it is to mourn that first
raw flush of manhood in a son,
when I see these perfect specimens
of flesh and bone defy
the season to make something more
like love than war upon each other,
my mother's death returns to me
as mute, as dread, as bitter-keen
as the midnight of its happening.

Sex on a Plate

is how one of the dinner guests, who's having an affair
with our hostess, describes her flourless chocolate cake.
Too dry, she protests, conjuring a lake
of raspberry sauce and prompting him to empty his liqueur
glass over it, their eyes conjoining shamelessly
as smoke from a faulty damper insinuates the room.
Sparks like these no longer move
me to envy, or to recall my own erotic history.

This is my desire: To see my mother one
last time in her butter-yellow slacks and top;
to feel her small, age-softened body reach
for mine—knowing she has only months
to live—and the tensions love has sparked between us stop
pulling at us. To hear her call me *Peach.*

The Blue Blanket

1 Toward the end, my father argued
2 with my mother over everything: He wanted
3 her to eat again. He wanted her to take

4 her medicine. He wanted her
5 to live. He argued with her in their bed
6 at naptime. He was cold, he said,

7 tugging at the blanket tangled
8 in my mother's wasted limbs. From the hall
9 outside their room I listened

10 as love, caught and fettered, howled
11 at its captors, gnawing at its own flesh
12 in its frenzy to escape. Then I entered

13 without knocking, freed the blanket
14 trapped between my mother's knees and shook
15 it out once, high above

16 their bodies' cursive. It floated
17 for a moment, blue as the Italian sky
18 into which my father flew his bombs

19 in 1943, blue as the hat I'd bought her
20 for the winter she would never live
21 to see. My father's agitation eased,

22 my mother smiled up at me, her face
23 lucent with gratitude, as the blanket
24 sifted down on them like earth.

The Autumn House Poetry Series

OneOnOne
Jack Myers

Snow White Horses,
Selected Poems 1973-1988
Ed Ochester

The Leaving,
New and Selected Poems
Sue Ellen Thompson

Dirt
Jo McDougall

Fire in the Orchard
Gary Margolis

Just Once,
New and Previous Poems
Samuel Hazo

The White Calf Kicks
Deborah Slicer
2003 Autumn House Poetry Prize,
selected by Naomi Shihab Nye

The Divine Salt
Peter Blair

The Dark Takes Aim
Julie Suk

Satisfied with Havoc
Jo McDougall

Half Lives
Richard Jackson

Not God After All
Gerald Stern
with drawings by Sheba Sharrow

Dear Good Naked Morning
Ruth L. Schwartz
2004 Autumn House Poetry Prize,
selected by Alicia Ostriker

A Flight to Elsewhere
Samuel Hazo

Collected Poems
Patricia Dobler

The Autumn House
Anthology of Contemporary
American Poetry
edited by Sue Ellen Thompson

Déja Vu Diner
Leonard Gontarek

Lucky Wreck
Ada Limón
2005 Autumn House Poetry Prize,
selected by Jean Valentine

The Golden Hour
Sue Ellen Thompson

Woman in the Painting
Andrea Hollander Budy

Design and Production

Text and cover design by Kathy Boykowycz

Text set in ITC Garamond, designed in 1975 by Tony Stan

Printed by Thomson-Shore of Dexter, Michigan,
on Natures Natural, a 50% recycled paper